Let Yourself Be Loved

Phillip Bennett

Paulist Press
New York/Mahwah, New Jersey

Cover/book design and interior illustrations by Nicholas T. Markell.

Library of Congress Cataloging-in-Publication Data

Bennett, Phillip, 1952–
    Let yourself be loved / by Phillip Bennett.
        p.   cm. – (IlluminationBooks)
    Includes bibliographical references.
    ISBN 0-8091-3736-4 (alk. paper)
    1. God–Love. 2. Fear–Religious aspects–Christianity. 3. Spiritual life–Catholic Church. 4. Catholic Church–Doctrines. 5. Bennett, Phillip, 1952–   . I Title. II. Series.
BT140.B46   1997
231′.6–dc21   97-21394
                                                                CIP

Published by Paulist Press
997 Macarthur Boulevard
Mahwah, New Jersey 07430

Printed and bound in the
United States of America

Contents

Dedication

To Joseph Schaller:

"Truly, to see your face is to see the face of God."

IlluminationBooks

A Foreword

W hen this series was launched in 1994, I wrote that Illumination-Books were conceived to "bring to light wonderful ideas, helpful information, and sound spirituality in concise, illustrative, readable, and eminently practical works on topics of current concern."

In keeping with this premise, among the first books were offerings by well-known authors Joyce Rupp *(Little Pieces of Light...Darkness and Personal Growth)* and Basil Pennington *(Lessons from the Monastery That Touch Your Life)*. In addition, there were titles by up-and-coming authors and experts in the fields of spirituality and psychology. These books covered a wide array of topics: joy, controlling stress and anxiety, personal growth, discernment, caring for others, the mystery of the Trinity, celebrating the woman you are, and facing your own desert experiences.

The continued goal of the series is to provide great ideas, helpful steps, and needed inspiration in small volumes. Each of the books offers a new opportunity for the reader to explore possibilities and embrace practicalities that can be employed in everyday life. Thus, among the new and noteworthy themes for readers to discover are these: how to be more receptive to the love in our lives, simple ways to structure a personal day of recollection, a creative approach to enjoy reading sacred scriptures, and spiritual and psychological methods of facing discouragement.

Like the IlluminationBooks before them, forthcoming volumes are meant to be a source of support—without requiring an inordinate amount of time or prior preparation. To this end, each small work stands on its own. The hope is that the information provided not only will be nourishing in itself but also will encourage further exploration in the area.

When we view the world through spiritual eyes, we appreciate that sound knowledge is really useful only when it can set the stage for *metanoia,* the conversion of our hearts. Each of the IlluminationBooks is designed to contribute in some small but significant way to this process. So, it is with a sense of hope and warm wishes that I offer this particular title and the rest of the series to you.

–Robert J. Wicks
General Editor, IlluminationBooks

A Note from the Author

*I*n these pages I draw upon my own experiences as well as the experiences of those I have been privileged to journey with as pastor and pastoral psychotherapist. In all cases I have disguised identifying information to protect others' confidentiality. I have shared my written vignettes with those whose stories I tell, receiving their suggestions and final approval. I am deeply grateful for their permission to share parts of their story. Special thanks to Bob Wicks who invited me to write this book and to Maria Maggi, my editor, who has been so supportive and helpful all along the way. For so many whose lives have formed the rich tapestry of love and support from which these reflections have come. For my colleagues in the Neumann College Graduate Program in Pastoral Counseling and Spiritual Direction: Joann Wolski Conn, Eileen Flanagan, Suzanne Mayer, IHM, and Wally Fletcher. For my mentors and guides along the journey especially Benedict Reid, O.S.B., Ann Ulanov, James Hollis, Polly Young-Eisendrath, Beverley Zabriskie, and Howard Friend. And for those whose love has sustained me in a special way: for my mother and my father, for Charles Moore, and for Joseph Schaller.

—*Phillip Bennett, Ph.D.*

Introduction

The Love That Casts Out All Fear

"*There is no fear in love, but perfect love casts out fear; for fear has to do with punishment, and whoever fears has not yet reached perfection in love.*" —1 *John 4:18-19*

When I was twenty-two, I felt an urgency to decide my vocational future—an urgency not yet tempered by enough life experience to know that our most important life decisions often find us in unexpected ways. I wanted to know exactly what God's will for me was—now! While on retreat at a monastery, I met a monk named Benedict whom I enlisted in my anxious search for God's will. He listened patiently as I spun out my concerns about finding the path God wanted me to take. When I had finished my stream of questions and confusions, he let a comfortable silence settle around us. Finally he responded: "As you describe your search for God's will, this image comes to me: God is like a tape recorder full of instructions which you are trying to follow. But the tape recorder is in the next room with the door ajar and it is hard to make out all the words. You are trying to decipher what God is saying but you are always a beat or two behind and so you can never be sure you've got it exactly right."

The image jolted me. I had never thought of my quest to know God's will in this way. It seemed so inherently frustrating and anxious. Then Benedict suggested an alternative image: "Imagine that God wants, more than anything, simply to be with you and delight in your presence. When you pray, instead of trying to listen to that tape recorder in the next room, sit in a chair and imagine God in a chair right next to you. Just let yourself be in God's presence, without any agenda. Let God love you. See what happens."

Part of me found his suggestion wonderfully attractive, but another part of me thought it was too easy. Was God really this friendly and easy-going? Despite my misgivings, I took Benedict's advice and began "just sitting" in God's presence. In the silence I tried to imagine God wanting to be with me, enjoying my presence. But I soon discovered that I did not enjoy my own presence during these awkward sessions of silence. Without an agenda to focus on, all my mental demons began to rise up: restlessness, doubts (I wondered if God even existed), sadness, guilt, fear, anxiety, lack of self-love, anger, a need to control—they were all churning up as I struggled to imagine a loving God by my side.

After several days of "just sitting," very slowly, very subtly, I began to feel a Presence with me; a gentle, steady love that delighted in being with me. The Presence stirred delicately around the edge of my awareness but would seem to recede if I tried to catch a direct glimpse of it. If I tried to clutch it, analyze it, make it do my bidding, it quickly vanished from my awareness. But when I relaxed and gave up trying to make something happen, I again experienced the Presence holding me, sustaining me, loving me in wordless silence. It felt like a force both outside me and within me—a great, inexhaustible power, yet intimately near and gentle. I had begun praying in order to seek and find God, but instead I was discovering that God was seeking and finding me. I had set out to discover God's specific plan for my life—as if it were some divine blueprint. Instead I was discovering another understanding of God's "will"—God's longing to draw me ever closer in intimate love and delight.

The wonderful news my friend Benedict brought me was that God truly delights in me—as I am. God enjoys being with me as friends and lovers delight in being with each other. There are times when I am aware of God's love for me and my life feels like a duet danced with the Divine Lover. But more often my awareness of love's presence fades and I act as if my life is a solo act. This fluctuating awareness of God's presence seems to be a normal and inevitable part of our human experience. We cannot hold onto our experiences of grace; they touch us from beyond our comprehension and control, coming to us as unbidden gifts, surprising breakthroughs.

It is now more than twenty years since my first awareness of the Presence as I sat in the silence. It is still not easy for me simply to let myself be loved by God. I find lots of reasons to avoid the all-embracing Presence: I seek distractions, I turn my prayer into a project, I wander off in fantasies and planning. Like a fidgety child who climbs in and out of a parent's lap, I want God to hold me but then I pull away. I do and I don't want to let myself be loved unconditionally. This inner ambivalence is, as both theologians and psychologists tell us, a normal part of the human experience. We long for love and yet part of us fears it. In our reaching out to God and to others we are never completely of one mind: we can feel both love and hate, approach and avoidance, eager passion and cooling distance. We want to be known yet we also want to hide; what most attracts us also scares us the most. Accepting our ambivalence toward God and other people can help free us from an unrealistic perfectionism in which we expect ourselves to be without doubts and resistance to love. Knowing that our hearts are never completely undivided and free of anxiety allows us to accept the variety of hopes and fears that well up within us as a normal part of our humanity.

Despite all our continued resistance, unconditional love is always there waiting for us. When we have run through our many ways of resisting, love is there with arms outstretched, waiting to embrace us as we are. When we complicate our lives by imagining problems that never come to pass, love is there to untangle the gnarled web of our anxieties. When we play our mental movies of imagined glory—or failure—love is there as the solid Ground right beneath our feet, inviting us to take the next step back into reality. When we discover in our hearts a mysterious sadness, an unexpected anger, a vague, unnameable fear, love is there with us—not to take away the feeling but to meet us in it; to lead us through it into a deeper acceptance of ourselves and others. As we open daily to the love that surrounds us, we become increasingly sure that we can trust this love to be there, no matter what life may bring.

In my work as a parish priest and pastoral psychotherapist I have had the great privilege of hearing many people share their experiences of God's unconditional acceptance. In prayer and study groups, in hospitals, in my consulting room, people tell moving stories about being touched by Love. Often they are initially embarrassed and cautious about telling their story, unsure whether their spiritual experiences are valid, normal, or authentic. They frequently defer to clergy and other religious professionals as the "spiritual experts." But in the spiritual life there are no experts, only beginners. As people realize their religious experiences will not be judged, amazing stories of their encounters with God emerge. These encounters may be quite dramatic or they may be quite simple. Whatever the particulars, I have always found these stories deeply moving. As I listen, I am convinced afresh of the power of God's love to touch us exactly at our point of need.

A woman I will call Margaret (all the names I use will be fictitious) told of an experience she had while cleaning her basement. "I was alone in the basement by myself cleaning. I felt a heaviness in my heart, thinking about someone in my family who was seriously ill. I remember so clearly the exact moment when it happened—I was sweeping the basement steps, watching the broom swinging back and forth. Suddenly, for no apparent reason, I looked up and I stood there—I don't know how long—with my eyes lighting on every detail in the basement: the sink with water dripping, the hum of the furnace, the piles of clothes and toys. Suddenly I realized I was not alone; there was a presence with me, a very tender presence that was drawing near to me, sharing my pain, comforting me. Then a great wave of love broke over me and I burst into tears of joy. As this love washed over me, I knew with deep certainty that this love had always been with me and would always be with me, no matter what happened to me or my loved ones. I also knew that this love extended to every person, every animal, plant, every particle of the universe. I stood at the bottom of the basement steps with the broom in my hand, weeping for joy."

Unexpectedly, love had broken into Margaret's daily awareness. Although the emotional intensity and poignancy of the encounter has faded into the background of her awareness, it is now a powerful touchstone for her, always somewhere close to consciousness, reminding her that she is not alone, that she and everyone she meets is loved with the wonderful, all-embracing love that flooded her heart as she stood on her basement steps.

An experience of God's unconditional acceptance such as Margaret's basement epiphany takes time to integrate into everyday life. As the beauty of the experience fades, we often find it hard to sustain an awareness of God's loving presence; something in us pulls away; we become distracted, even resistant to an awareness of being loved. It is then that we need some regular spiritual practice to recollect us to God's presence. By placing ourselves intentionally in the presence of unconditional love—through prayer, meditation, reading, serving others—we return to the mysterious Center beyond our ego control and comprehension which alone can calm our fears and ground us deeply in reality. In subtle ways we find ourselves becoming more loving, less fearful and grasping. Slowly, like water wearing down a stone, the steady drops of love are washing away our fears. As we place ourselves daily under the stream of divine mercy, the living waters of love flow through us, slowly penetrating our fearful, dark recesses. The change that is wrought within us is gradual but deep; slow and subtle, but always profound.

The lessons of love take a lifetime of learning. No one is a graduate, for there is no final point of arrival. No one ever moves completely beyond the ambivalence and ambiguity of our human experience into some anxiety-free state of certainty. The process of learning to be loved and to love is messy, unpredictable, spontaneous and surprising. There is no perfect way to do it; all that matters is to keep loving and allowing ourselves to be loved. Our attempts at chiseling away our own anxieties and distractions never succeed, but we are promised that the fullness of love alone can cast out our fears (John 3:10). This casting out continues over our lifetime, and perhaps even after our death as we enter ever more fully into the presence of Love.

Let us now look at some of the fears which keep us from letting ourselves be loved. These fears I discuss are not an exhaustive list, nor are they neatly separable into distinct categories. Usually we find them jumbled together in a confusing welter. Our fears often arise in our psychological blind-spots, making it difficult to recognize their power and persistence. But as we open ourselves to love and continue in our spiritual practice, we come, in time, to see our fears more clearly. As we grow more conscious of our besetting fears, the key is not to judge them or try too hard to get rid of them. If we try to run from them or eradicate them, we only give them more power. Instead, we need to extend to the fearful parts of ourselves the same kind of compassion and patience we would extend to someone we love. Only by befriending the fears in our hearts do we give up trying to control them and simply open our hearts so that love may work its deep healing within us.

Chapter One

The Fear of Opening Old Wounds

W*e must come to love our wounds.*
—Friedrich Nietzsche

Lucia, a woman in my former parish, was diagnosed with liver cancer in her mid 50's. She was an intensely private person, with a thick emotional shell that kept others from getting too close. She was respected for her efficiency at work and in her volunteer duties at the church but she had little social life. When not at work or at church, she retreated to her small efficiency apartment where she lived as a recluse.

But then came the cancer. Little by little she began to risk reaching out to a few people in the parish. As she let them know of her cancer, people offered their

support. But as soon as she opened the door to let someone into her life, she slammed it shut in the person's face. Lucia was fortunate to be surrounded by people who were ready to love her for the long haul, even when she tried to reject their love and return to her isolation.

Love pierces to the core of who we are. And where love touches us to the core, it also touches the pain we carry inside us. What I did not know until her last days was that Lucia had suffered a great wounding from love. As a young woman, she had been engaged to a Protestant seminarian who suddenly broke off the engagement with little explanation. Lucia was sent reeling, and in her hurt and anger she pulled inside herself and shut the door. Like Charles Dickens' Miss Havisham in *Great Expectations*, she had locked her heart away where no one could touch it, mourning for a groom who would never come.

As the cancer worsened, Lucia had to quit her job, being stripped of her last bastion of self-definition. She was no longer valued for her efficiency and helpfulness; now she was the one being helped. After several hospital stays, members of the parish convinced her to come home and let them provide round-the-clock hospice care. Her already slender body became increasingly frail and her skin and eyes grew more jaundiced each day. Although she seemed less resistant to being cared for, she still kept her suit of armor in place even as her privacy and health were being stripped away.

The summer came and Lucia continued her slow decline. I had just returned from vacation, not having seen her for several weeks. She was now almost a skeleton. But it was not her withered body that caught my eye as I walked into her room—it was her *eyes*. They were fully alive, completely open channels through which I could see right into her. And she was looking directly into me. There were no longer any walls, no more shame or fear. I was so stunned that the first thing I said was, "Lucia, what's happened to you?" A broad, radiant smile broke across her face. She replied, "I finally let God love me! I really know God loves me and that other people love me!" I could see the love welling up in her eyes. She was a transformed person, radiant, on fire, even as her body was passing away.

Lucia's funeral was like no other I remember, for everyone who had gathered around her had seen the fire in her eyes and knew it was love that had worked this amazing transformation. In her face we had seen the glory of God shining, showing us a foretaste of what was in store for all of us. The image of her radiant eyes continues to point the way for me, reminding me that when I let down my walls, love can work miracles of transformation.

Whether we resist until our death like Lucia, or open up earlier in life, the challenge is the same for all of us: to choose the pain of opening up old wounds over the pain of sealing them off. Either way we will experience pain. We will, as T.S. Eliot said, be "consumed by either fire or fire."[1] The fire of fear makes our life a living hell of isolation and unshared pain. But the fire of love cauterizes, heals and frees us.

Going into our pain can be frightening. The intensity of the hurt may feel as if it will overwhelm us. But if we close our hearts in order to avoid further hurt, we also close ourselves to the transforming power of love. We may need to find a trusted friend or a trained professional who can accompany us on our healing journey. When our moods become too intense or unstable, we should also consider medical help, because medication may help us considerably if there is a biological component to our suffering. Support and recovery groups can also provide safe places where we can share our stories of suffering and grace, discovering that our pain can become a bridge connecting us with others.

Pain, when embraced instead of denied, can become a precious gift which deepens our compassion for others. In novelist Frederick Buechner's words, we are called to be good "stewards of our pain,"[2] not burying our pain but investing it. In a mysterious way, sharing our pain instead of hiding it, can bring healing not only to ourselves but to those around us. Within the hidden pain often lie the seeds of new growth. The place where we are hurt is also the place where we can come to know love in new and surprising ways.

A friend of mine was leading her son's cub scout troop in a mask-making workshop. As the troop was busily at their task, she noticed one boy who seemed particularly intent as he leaned over his mask. She watched as he made cuts in the papier-mâché face and then carefully sprinkled colored glitter into the incisions. My friend watched him, intrigued, then finally asked him what he was doing. He looked up from his labors and told her, "The jewels are in the wounds." Out of the mouths of babes, indeed! It is out of our suffering that the riches of wisdom and compassion are formed. These jewels—like actual gems—usually take a long time to form and we cannot short-circuit the process. If we try too quickly to find the jewels in our wounds, we avoid descending fully into our pain, and are left with false jewels which may sparkle but lack solidity and richness. I remember how stunned I was by a former therapist's words to me: "I don't believe you have gotten to the bottom of your despair yet." I knew, in an instant, that she was right: I had been treading water over my feelings and needed to go into them and out the other end in order to be free of my fear of what was inside me. As I finally got to the bottom of my feelings of despair I realized I no longer had to run from them; they were a part of me but they did not have to have the last word. In time I came to appreciate the great wealth hidden in my suffering; I could use my experience to help understand my clients' apprehensions as they stared down into the swirling abyss of feelings inside them. Although my inner abyss and theirs are not exactly the same, I have some idea what it is to face the frightening places inside, not knowing for sure what the outcome will be. As we do battle with our demons and come out the other side, we become bearers of hope to others; our authority comes from our genuine encounter with our psychic depths. We, like Jacob, have wrestled with our dark angel and have received both a wound and a blessing. And in some paradoxical way, the wound actually becomes the blessing. No wonder, then, that the verb "to wound" in French is "blesser." When we have gone into the pain, instead of running from it, we discover new hope and compassion which has been forged in the fire of suffering. To the degree that we have embraced our pain, we, like Jesus, have descended into hell, have gone all the way down into our own darkness and despair and have come out the other side into the resurrection life.

The words "wound" and "wonder" share a common root which means "to penetrate." Our wounds are the places where life has penetrated us. These places can either become infected and closed off or they can become channels that open us to fuller life and love. As we experience the healing power of love, we do not merely survive our wounds: we are shaped by them and find new energy in them. Many of us in helping professions would never have developed our sensitivity to others' pain if we had not suffered ourselves. Truly effective helpers are those who have walked the same road as those they are helping. As Henri Nouwen reminds us, genuine healers are always wounded healers who find in their own wounds reservoirs of compassion and wisdom from which they can draw when ministering to others.[3] As we experience healing, our wounds never really go away; instead, as they heal they become deep wells within in us in which we may feel the pain of the world and respond, not with the hollow optimism of those who run from their suffering, but as those who have learned to trust a healing power at work even in the bleakest hours of life. The Risen Christ never loses his wounds, even in his resurrection body. His wounded hands, feet and side identify him to his loved ones; they are the unmistakable signs that he has been through death and has returned victorious. So too with us: our wounds become signs of hope to others that it is possible to die and rise again, to come out the other side of suffering and despair.

Prayer

O God,
for so long I hid my wounds
both from myself and others,
feeling ashamed, isolated,
secretly hopeless
that they could be healed.
Now I can see how deeply
my wounds unite me to every person
and to all of life.
We all suffer,
we are all wounded by life.
Thank you that my wounds
become channels of your grace
if I but trust your healing power.
Thank you that my wounds identify me—
just as the Risen Christ is known
by his glorious scars.
Although I once could not
have imagined it,
my wounds have become
something wonderful—
a bridge to life
instead of a barrier;
an inexhaustible
well of life
instead of a bottomless
abyss of despair.
Through my wounds
your love has penetrated
me to my core
and in them I have

mined the jewels of your grace.
For this unspeakable gift
I thank you with
an overflowing heart.
                    –*Phillip Bennett*

Chapter Two
The Fear of Judgment

"*This is for us the fullness of love, to have confidence on the day of judgment.... There is no room for fear in love; perfect love banishes fear, for fear brings with it the pains of judgment.*"

—1 John 4:17-18

The fear of judgment is a universal human condition. Even the most self-confident of us harbor secret doubts about ourselves—doubts about our worth, our accomplishments, our acceptability. These doubts are amazingly persistent despite all our attempts to reassure ourselves with "rational" estimations of our worth.

A man near forty whom I will call David is always

impeccably dressed for his therapy sessions. He is quite successful as an architect and is highly regarded in his field. Yet when he first came to see me for psychotherapy, David was tortured by self-judgment. He felt he was a boring, hollow person, trying unsuccessfully to con the world into believing he was interesting. His frequent refrain was, "If people could see into me and know how little there is inside, they would never want to spend time with me." He spoke of his "demon" of self-judgment who sat on his shoulder whispering harsh, despairing messages. Our work was long and slow, helping him to realize that his "critical demon" need not have the final word. One evening he went to a party and was surprised and delighted to enjoy himself without his demon ruining everything. He was animated as he described this new experience: "I had this glimpse of really liking myself, of knowing I'm a worthwhile person. It came and went, but at least I felt it briefly." Predictably, it wasn't long before his demon of self-judgment came swooping down again: "Whom are you trying to kid? You can't sustain this kind of spontaneity; you'll always be this way; stop trying to fight it." This self-judging voice was still fierce, but now there was another competing voice which David dubbed his Good Demon. He imagined his warring demons sitting on either shoulder, whispering their conflicting messages in his ear. As David felt increasingly more alive and less self-judging, his Bad Demon shrank and his Good Demon grew stronger.

One day David shared a memory of golf balls he and his brother collected when they were boys. They lived next to a golf course and spent free time combing the area for stray balls. David had always imagined that the golf balls were hollow at their core. Finally he and his brother broke one open, unwinding the rubber bands inside: "It seemed like miles of this rubber band-like material. I was sure we would find a hollow center when we unwound this mass of rubber string. But I was surprised to find this very small but dense core at the center. I see that golf ball as a metaphor for my self: I used to be afraid to unwrap all the layers inside me for fear that I would find an empty core. But instead I've found myself, and it's solid. It's such a relief. I want to tell other people who feel hollow and worthless that they really are worthwhile. Thank God I've finally been able to experience this solid part of myself."

David had touched a core in himself which was not of his own making and therefore beyond his judgment. He was lovable because he was made in the image of love. As the battle between the two demons increased, David began to talk explicitly about spiritual concerns, describing how he had prayed to find a way through his fear and lack of self-confidence: "Recently I did something I haven't done since I was a child: I got down on my knees and prayed to God, saying, "I want to feel fully alive. I want to feel it all—the joy and the pain."

David was discovering his self-worth not only as other people mirrored it back to him, but as Being itself mirrored it to him. Only this affirmation from Ultimate Being could free him from his crippling dependence on validation from others or himself. David's experience of a solid inner core resonates with many of the great spiritual teachers who image God residing at the center of the human soul.[4] Only by returning continually to this unshakable center of Being within us can we find freedom from our withering self-judgment.

Why do we feel these self-judgments even when the more rational part of ourselves knows we are all right as we are? In his "Self Psychology" psychoanalyst Heinz Kohut[5] describes how we develop our sense of self through our early interactions with others. As children, others mirror back to us our existence and worth. People hold us, talk to us, play with us, praise us, and so let us know we are important and lovable. In time, children internalize the mirroring they receive from others, carrying their own inner sense of worth. Our self-esteem comes from being esteemed by others and taking that esteem into ourselves. But our need for mirroring and validation does not end with childhood. Even the most self-confident person needs continual validation throughout life; we can never get enough affirmation. But because our need for validation is endless we face a dilemma when we continue to seek it only from other people or from possessions or accomplishments, for all these sources can give us only a partial and transitory affirmation. In time—if we are honest with ourselves—we discover, with Augustine of Hippo, that our hearts are, indeed, restless until they find their rest in God. God alone has an unlimited capacity to mirror our own worth to us and give us the continual affirmation we need, even to our dying breath. This does not mean that affirmation from other people is not important or can be side-stepped by going to God. That would be to misuse our spiritual practice as a way of avoiding the messy and transforming experience of human love. But we must also come to realize that other people are not God; they can only give us partial affirmation. Our relationships are meant to circle around a greater Center to whom we must all turn for unconditional love. When we are in touch with this Center we are free to love each other deeply without possessiveness, realizing we have been given to each other as equals, fellow travelers, all returning to our common Source for our ultimate identity.

Just as we must not look to others for our ultimate identity, so we must not look even to ourselves. In order to let ourselves be loved unconditionally by God, we must confront our strong attachment to our self-images. As the contemplative psychiatrist Gerald May reminds us, "attachment" comes from the old French "nailed to": when we take our self-images as the final word about ourselves, we feel we have ourselves nailed down, defined, understood.[6] We think we really *are* these images and either cling to the positive ones (attachment) or run from the negative ones (aversion). But to the degree that we run toward or away from these self-images we lose our freedom simply to *be*, without judgments or conditions. Both running toward and running away from these images limit our inner freedom and alienate us from Being. Although "positive" self-images may seem more helpful, they bring only temporary relief from our insecurity and self-doubt because living up to our own positive self-images can be as exhausting and enslaving as our negative self-images. In fact, these positive self-images can set us up for self-judgment: when we do not live up to our own expectations we find ourselves suddenly deflated, depressed and self-judging. In Kohut's terms we oscillate between a "grandiose" self-image which is too big, too good, too shaky, and the "narcissistic injury" that comes when that grandiose image is punctured. For example, we may pride ourselves on being loving and sensitive, strongly needing others to see us this way. But when we are criticized for being uncaring, it feels devastating, as if our whole identity is being challenged and undermined.

As we cling to our self-images we are bound in a continual cycle of inflation and deflation, unable to rest simply in being ourselves without categories and judgments. The liberating truth we need to hear is that our worth and identity have nothing to do with our positive or negative self-representations. They are *not* our true identity, no matter how real and substantial they may seem to us. Our true identity can only be found in our Loving Creator who has created us for intimate relationship. Only as we return to the One who is at the core of our being can we find release from the self-images which we cling to or run from. There is a great paradox here: we must empty ourselves of our carefully constructed "selves" in order to be filled with the fullness of our true self. We must release our fierce grip on our self-created identity in order to discover our identity in Being. As we loosen our attachment to our self-images, we are met by God who is already within us, waiting to embrace and affirm us as we are. We discover that we are *already* validated, simply for being ourselves, for being alive.

Given the destructive nature of our self-judgment, what are we to make of all the images of *God's* judgment in our religious scriptures and traditions? How can we reconcile God's love with God's judgment? The most satisfying answer I have found is that God's judgment *is* God's love, in its penetrating, unremitting power. God's judgment is never divorced from God's love; it is not some angry part of God which is split off from God's mercy and gentleness. Instead, God's judgment is the way we experience pure and constant love which sees and knows us to our core. Being known so deeply is like David's golf ball: our layers of self-deception and avoidance of intimacy must be unwound until love can touch us to our core.

Sometimes we fear that God's judgment will hurt us. We have difficulty imagining that God will not inflict the same hurt and shame on us that we have inflicted on ourselves or have suffered at the hands of others. In C.S. Lewis' *The Voyage of the Dawn Treader,*[7] the sour and willful boy Eustace strays off by himself and finds a cave full of golden jewelry. Unbeknownst to him, the cave and jewelry belong to a dragon he has just seen die. Eustace greedily grabs the most beautiful piece of jewelry, a large golden bracelet, and slides it on his arm. He then drifts off to sleep beside a fire in the dragon's cave. He awakens to an excruciating pain in his upper arm, for where there had been human flesh, Eustace now has dragon flesh and the

bracelet is cutting into his swollen, scaly body. Finally he meets up with Aslan the lion who assures him he can pierce Eustace's dragon body with his claws, just far enough to cut through the dragon flesh without hurting the little boy within. This is a great test for Eustace and for each of us: trusting that the penetrating judgment of God's love will cut just far enough to remove all the tough scales we have grown around us to protect us from pain without damaging our true selves that lie beneath.

God's judgment is the penetrating aspect of God's love, purging, purifying, stripping away tough old skin. The judgment of love never injures our true self; it only releases it from constriction so that we may be the person we were created to be.

Prayer

My God,
a voice within me sometimes
judges me harshly.
I lose touch with that
solid core of goodness within me
which comes from you.
When I am seduced by
images of myself that
inflate or deflate,
help me return to you,
the core of my being.
Be my mirror
in which I may
behold myself undistorted,
seen through
the eyes of your love.
Help me know that
your judgment is always
the other side of your love;
the purging fire of your
infinite compassion
drawing me
and all creation
to yourself.

–Phillip Bennett

Chapter Three
The Fear of Loss

I *am lavish with riches made from loss.*
—May Sarton

There is no way to love without opening ourselves to loss. To the degree that we love, we will surely have our hearts broken. Our physical death and all the deaths that precede it will separate us from those we love. Loss is inevitable but the way we respond to it is not. When our hearts are broken, we may become bitter and rigid, unwilling to risk loving again. Or, we may choose—and what a hard choice it is!—to let our hearts be broken *open*, feeling our natural anger and desire to withdraw but deciding not to close our hearts to love. Our willingness to be broken open presumes some basic trust in life, for in order to let go we have to believe that something or someone will catch us as we fall. To the degree we have not felt secure in our past relationships, it is very hard to give ourselves fully in intimacy for fear that the pain of loss will eclipse the joy of loving.

In his writings on parent-child attachment, the English psychiatrist John Bowlby speaks of the importance of having a "secure base" from which to move into the world with confidence.[8] If a child experiences early love and reliability from parents, a "secure attachment" develops which allows the child to face unknown or fearful situations with an awareness of being loved and protected. But without this secure attachment, the child is prone to separation anxiety, or may be unable to form any deep attachments at all. Although our early relationships strongly shape us, Bowlby believes that as adults we may still be able to make up for the secure base we didn't get early in life by finding people who can provide the nurturing and reliability we need. But no matter how satisfying our human attachments are, they never provide us with an absolutely secure base. Here Bowlby's ideas, like Kohut's, do not address the need for a source of support and validation beyond human relationships. No matter how satisfying our human attachments, they never provide us with an absolutely secure base. Consequently, separation anxiety can be more than a developmental arrest; it can signal a deep awareness of life's fragility and the inevitable separations which await us all. We *will* be separated, sooner or later, from those we love; in this sojourn on earth there is truly no abiding place.

Without God as our secure base, our love of others easily becomes distorted by our fear of loss: we cling to others for fear of losing them (which may, in fact, drive them away, fulfilling our worst fear). Or we may try to avoid the pain of loss by avoiding intimacy altogether. Whatever our particular defense against loss, it is only when we return to the ground of our being, the Center from which we come and to which we return, that we can be freed to love others without making them false centers of our life; idols we clutch in a vain attempt to ward off separation and loss. The secure base of God's love will not take away our losses but it can help us discover an abiding Presence that sustains us even in the midst of things that are passing away. In letting ourselves be loved by God, we form an attachment to the only One who cannot leave us.

Times of loss and disequilibrium confront us with a world beyond our control and comprehension. Like Alice in Wonderland falling down the rabbit hole, the familiar and dependable collapse under us and we lose our balance and fall, not knowing where we will land. At first Alice is afraid that she will never land; then she is afraid she will land and be destroyed on impact. I remember a time of loss in my own life when I felt as though I were falling down a rabbit hole. My trust in life was shaken; I was profoundly disillusioned. How could God allow this to happen? What had seemed like solid ground was suddenly collapsing underneath me like a trap door. I felt as though I was free-falling down a dark tunnel, plummeting into the unknown. As I fell, I sent out a desperate prayer: "God, if

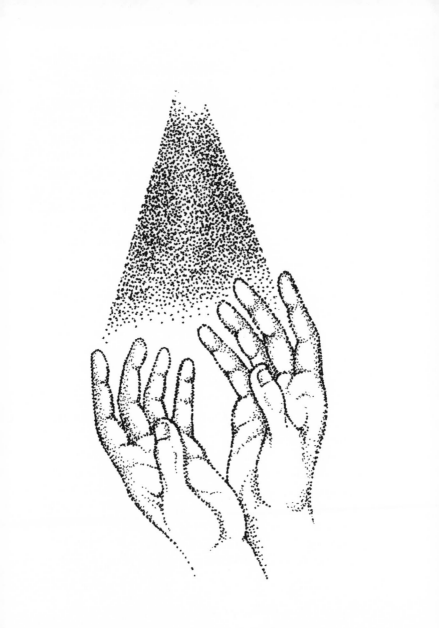

you are there, let me know and feel your presence. I can no longer make myself believe. I am letting go, but I am not sure if you will be there to catch me." As I fell through inner space, I felt the terror of letting go of all my preconceived ideas about how things should be; I let go of everything I had been trying to sustain through my own power. After a dizzying time of free-fall I suddenly felt a jolt: I was being caught and held by Loving Hands. There was Someone out there besides myself! Someone bigger than my doubts and fears who was now meeting me exactly at the point of my helplessness and need. I knew this was not my own doing. I had hit rock bottom—and it was Love.

Of course this was not my last fall down the rabbit hole! Periodically the ground rumbles beneath my feet and I realize that my world is once again opening up. It is time again to fall further into the mystery of life. But with each new fall, I carry with me the memory of God's sustaining presence. Although I may feel frightened and disoriented, a voice within tells me that this loss, too, can be another fall into grace.

When we experience loss—of a loved one, of health, of a job, a familiar way of life—the pain is tremendous. There is no way to short-circuit our grief; it comes in waves which only gradually lessen in intensity. Grief cannot be rushed even when those around us may wish it shortened to ease their own discomfort. But over time our loss begins to give us hidden riches: a gratitude for every precious moment of life; a sense that all is a gift to be treasured; a deepened empathy for others. These are not riches we have chosen; they, like our losses, have come unbidden, unexpectedly. In her recent interview with the radio talk show host and psychologist Dan Gottlieb, psychologist and Jungian analyst Polly Young-Eisendrath records Dan's description of how others were instinctively drawn to him for comfort and support after his car accident which left him a quadriplegic:

> I found some barrier between me and others had disappeared. I remember talking to people in intimate ways in my hospital room, and just floating inside of them and knowing what it was like to be them, and knowing how they felt. A lot of people would come to see me and say they didn't know why they were coming. It wasn't about their guilt or compulsions or any of that crap. There was something pulling them there and I think it was because of the way I talked and listened to them.[9]

As we find new depths of meaning even while we still ache with loss, others begin to see the riches in us; they recognize in us someone who has suffered and so can understand their losses without giving words of false comfort.

In Frederick Buechner's novel *Godric,* the twelfth century holy man Godric is a much coarser and more complex mix of sinner and saint than his friend and biographer Reginald depicts him to be. As Reginald is reading portions of his sanitized biography to the aging hermit, Godric chokes to hear himself described as "this saint."

"This SAINT! I cry...Blasphemer! Fool!"[10] Then Godric has a stroke which renders him speechless and paralyzed. Another friend, Perkin, hoists Godric's hand up so he may bless his own biography before he dies. As he slips from life to death, Godric says this mute farewell:

> Sweetheart, have pity.
> Perkin, hoist my hand again.
> All's lost. All's found.
> Farewell.[11]

In this fleeting life ultimately all *is* lost. Our loves, our labors, our hopes and dreams, all are carried away by the river of death. But in letting go of what we cannot keep from losing, we, with Godric, discover that all that is lost is also found again. All our farewells are somehow gathered into the heart of Love where they are redeemed and made a gateway into a life that is fuller, richer, more joyful than anything we could have imagined. In some way too mysterious for us to comprehend, even loss is the entrance into life. The risen Christ startles us as we look up with tear-stained faces. "It is I; do not be afraid. Your mourning has been turned to joy."

Prayer

My God,
I can never prepare myself for loss;
it is always wrenching,
disorienting.
But help me to trust
that each loss can teach me
not to cling so tightly;
to let go, to fall
into the unknown
where you lie waiting
to meet me.
All will be lost:
my loved ones,
my body, my life.
But you have promised
that all that is lost
will be found again in you.
Help me find the riches
hidden in my loss,
the rock-certainty of your love
in the swirling rapids of change.
Help me to lose
that I may gain.
May all my losses
lead me back to you.

–Phillip Bennett

Chapter Four

The Fear of Merger

"True union does not confound but differentiates."
        —Teilhard de Chardin

Allowing ourselves to be loved can trigger another fear of loss—the fear of losing *ourselves*. Instead of fearing that the other will disappear, we fear that *we* will disappear, being swallowed up in the intensity of the relationship. Martha, a woman in her late thirties, described it this way: "I want an intimate relationship so badly, but when I start getting close to someone, I become obsessed with him. It's as though I can't live without him. I start to plan my life around what I imagine he wants or doesn't want. The deeper I go into the relationship, the more I

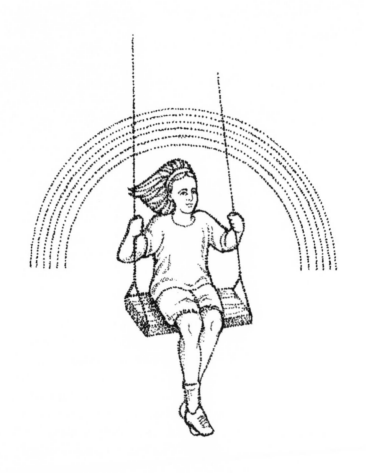

lose my relationship with myself. Then I start to panic and pull back in order to feel separate. That's when I usually bail out." In her family she had found no reliable balance between separateness and connection; people were either too close or too far away. As usually happens, her image of God had been shaped by her family relationships: she experienced God as either invasive or distant.

Martha's dilemma points to the inherent tension in all relationships: how can we maintain our sense of separateness while also making intimate connection with others? The British pediatrician and psychoanalyst D.W. Winnicott speaks of a child's developing capacity to "be alone in the presence of another."[12] As children become more independent, they "practice" being alone, absorbed in their own activity, but always with some reliable adult presence nearby. Periodically, children run back to mother or father to show the fruits of their activity. The key, says Winnicott, is for the adult neither to impinge on the child's own space, nor to abandon or ignore the child.

Winnicott's idea has rich implications for our relationship with God. Can we feel free simply to be ourselves in God's presence, trusting that God will allow us to relax and be ourselves without either impinging on us or abandoning us? When my own prayer began to shift from an anxious attempt to find out "what God wanted from me" to a growing trust that God simply wanted to *be* with me without any agenda, I was learning simply to "be alone in the presence of another." In not censoring my thoughts or trying to "please" God, I was discovering I could be myself fully with a God who not only permitted but delighted in my freedom. This, says Winnicott, is what "good-enough" parents do; they allow children to play because they know they are safe. It is also what God does for us. Prayer, though often hard work, is also fundamentally an act of play, for it involves being ourselves in God's delighting presence.

When we fear merger—whether with another person or with God—we still imagine that we must make a choice to be either separate or connected. In fact this is always a false choice, for our connectedness depends on our separateness and our separateness depends on our connectedness. But too often families have what family systems therapist Murray Bowen calls a "stuck-togetherness" in which family members assume they must all think and feel the same way.[13] Individual differences are seen as threatening to the family unity. In this atmosphere of oppressive conformity, all disagreements must either be covered over with a false compliance, or a family member must make an "emotional cut-off," trying to put emotional and often physical distance between themselves and the family. But, says Bowen, the farther we run from our families, the more we are controlled by their emotional force field. Bowen believes we have a need for both individuality and togetherness, and when these two needs are balanced, we become "differentiated," able to maintain good relations both with ourselves and with others. Only by learning to speak our own truth non-reactively in love do we become more honest with our families while at the same time coming to accept (though not always to like) them as they are.

We all know what a long struggle it is to become more differentiated in our family of origin! A trip home shows us how hard it is to stay centered once we re-enter the old family force field. The first day we may do quite well, congratulating ourselves on how maturely we're handling our family. The second day a few old irritations surface, but we grit our teeth and bear them. As the days go by, we find ourselves regressing emotionally until we feel as if we are four or five years old! The old spontaneous reactions are returning; we find ourselves wanting to withdraw or attack. Our emotions are reverting to "automatic pilot" and our carefully rehearsed composure is cracking. We feel hemmed in, on edge, about to explode, ready to pack the car and leave in a grand gesture of self-assertion.

To the degree that we have not sufficiently differentiated from our family of origin, Bowen believes we keep playing out the same merger/flight issues in all our close relationships: in marriages, with children, in parishes and communities, in our relationship with God. When we experience extreme and persistent conflicts in any of these relationships, it is important to look back to our family of origin to see how the original "stuck-togetherness" may be affecting our present relationships. As we gain understanding of our family system and our own reactions, we are able to *react* less and to *respond* more.

Bowen's ideas fit well with the spiritual truth that the more intimate we are, the more our unique personhood is affirmed. Love does not merge us together with other people or God. Rather, love draws us into union where we become more fully ourselves, delighting in each other's individuality. This may be one of the hardest lessons of love for us to learn, but it is certainly one of the most important.

Prayer

My God,
in your Triune life
there is room for all.
You create us to be separate
yet deeply connected.
When my anxiety
moves me toward merger or flight,
help me to remember that
true union
joins without melding;
true autonomy
is rooted in interdependence.
Teach me that deep fidelity
to myself
is also fidelity to others
and to you.
O Spacious Intimacy,
teach me to love
so that I am neither too close
nor too far from others.
Draw me deeper into
this dance of love
where our distances touch
and our intimacy leaves
sacred space for all.

– Phillip Bennett

Chapter Five
The Fear of Self-Enlargement

"In the cosmos there is no refuge from change."

–Carl Sagan

Being loved unconditionally is a stretching experience. We realize this instinctively and so resist being the object of God's love. The Hebrew word for salvation, "yasha," means to "enlarge, to lead into a broad place." Although part of us longs for the spaciousness of salvation, another part clings to the narrowness of our neuroses and negativity. The Israelites cried for deliverance from their captivity in Egypt, but, once delivered, found their new freedom disconcerting and frightening. Slavery was oppressive but it was also predictable, for they knew their food and shelter were guaranteed. But in the vast, unfamiliar wilderness they were driven to a radical dependence on God, receiving manna only one day at a time. Letting ourselves be loved sets us on an exodus journey out of our self-captivity into the glorious liberty of the children of God, and, like all growth, this movement into freedom upsets our status quo and involves growing pains.

To the degree that we are unwilling to let go of our fixed view of ourself and the world, we find the spaciousness of God's love threatening. As long as we are the ones giving love, we can still feel in control. We initiate and direct. We "do something." But when we let ourselves be loved, we are doing "nothing"; we are naked, in need, the recipients of free and unearned love. It is easy to accept love if we believe we have "earned" it. In this way we can still receive love on our own terms, keeping ourselves at the center of our world. We may cling to our role as giver and so avoid confronting what Christian theologian Johannes Metz calls "poverty of spirit"[14]: an awareness that we cannot meet our own deepest desires through our own power. Only when we own our poverty and neediness and then feel the inflowing of a Power beyond ourselves can we understand that letting ourselves be loved is not selfish indulgence; it is absolutely necessary and the bedrock from which our own loving must flow.

Our awareness of being loved unconditionally by God has a profound effect on our everyday experience. When we lose touch with being loved, other people feel more distant to us, like strangers at the periphery of our

world. Even in our intimate relationships, others feel like they are "out there"—beyond our personal orbit of self-concern. But when we are aware of being loved, we realize there are never really any "strangers." We glimpse the infinite preciousness of every person, every creature, on this amazing planet. The veil of familiarity is stripped away and, at least for a fleeting moment, we can say of every person we meet what Jacob said as he was reunited with his estranged brother Esau: "Truly, to see your face is to see the face of God" (Genesis 33:10). This capacity to see into the heart of things as God sees is a precious gift of the Spirit which calls us beyond our narrow, self-protective shell. Throughout the day there are countless opportunities either to retreat into our shell or to reach out, to enlarge our perspective. When we have withdrawn into our protective shells, we harbor the illusion of being in control, of being at a safe remove. We think we know exactly who our friends and enemies are. But life in the shell takes its toll, for we must always defend what is "ours" while keeping a "safe" distance between ourselves and others. But as we open to the radical inclusiveness of love, we realize there is room to be ourselves *and* to let others into our lives on a deep level. Love is a paradox which clarifies and deepens both our individuality and our communion with all of life.

The action of God's love is often said to produce a capacity in us for "self-transcendence." I am uneasy with this phrase because it can imply rising above or beyond ourselves, of being "less" human and "more" divine. The image of enlarging ourselves does not imply leaving ourselves but of being stretched by the vastness of God who comes to dwell in our humanity and make us incarnations of love. Where the Spirit of Love runs free, life is stretched beyond the familiar, filled to overflowing with vitality and joy. As we become increasingly aware of God's love for us, we begin to see others, and all creation, through the eyes of love. Our fearful and constricted hearts begin to open to the joyful awareness that there is more than enough love to go around, that no one is more deserving of love than another. Although this is ultimately a joyful change, it also stretches us, calling us to move beyond our self-absorption, to break out of our familiar ruts, to sojourn into the spaciousness of a new and unfamiliar land.

We ask God for many things: for healing, guidance, understanding. God gives us not only the answers to our prayers, but also God's self. We are reluctant to accept this amazing gift because we realize it requires a response in kind. So we try to keep God at a comfortable distance, hoping we can avoid the crucible of intimate encounter. But like all human intimacy, we cannot love God without approaching the "consuming fire" (Hebrews 12:29). A Hasidic Jewish saying puts it this way: "God is not 'nice'; God is an earthquake!" The divine Presence shakes our foundations, opens us up, upsets our neat personal universes which we guard with fierce vigilance. Perhaps this is why we find all sorts of excuses for avoiding prayer; something in us knows that spending time with God will force us to confront our own desire to remain in complete control.

We want and don't want God's love. And so, with the English poet John Donne we must cry, "Batter my heart, Three-Personed God,"[15] offering to God our divided and ambivalent hearts. This offering of our mixed desires is all we can do, or need to do, for we will never resolve our ambivalence in this life. There is no "perfect" surrender to be attained, only starting over again and again. There is no score to be kept, only the endless drawing of Love, which invites us anew each day to discover the secret grace in loosening our tight grip on life, the surprising joy that comes when we learn—yet again—that we are not in ultimate control.

Biblical scholar J.B. Phillips wrote a book entitled, *Your God Is Too Small,* in which he described our tendency to reduce God to our own little frames of reference.[16] We could extend his phrase and add "and so your self is too small" because we try to shrink both God and ourselves in an attempt to avoid the uncomfortable vastness of mystery. Because we are made in God's image we are always more mysterious, more vast than our attempts at self-understanding and self-mastery will allow. As we open to the inflowing of love, we discover new "elbow room" to let ourselves and others simply *be*—without tidy categories and either/or choices. With the psalmist we can exclaim: "It was you who created my inmost self, and put me together in my mother's womb; for all these mysteries I thank you: for the wonder of myself, for the wonder of your works" (Psalm 139:13-14).

Prayer

My God,
sometimes I do not want to grow,
to move forward in freedom,
to leave my comfortable captivity.
I cling to the familiar smallness
of my old world,
pulling back from the
vast wilderness of the exodus journey.
Help me to open to the
stretching of your Spirit;
to allow my heart
to be expanded beyond my
immediate comfort and control.
Lead me into that larger life,
that wide land of plenty
where my narrow self
can blossom with new life.
Enlarge my heart, O God;
fill me with your
boundless love.

−Phillip Bennett

Chapter Six
The Fear of Loving Ourselves

"*As you love yourself, so must you love your neighbor.*"
— *Matthew 19:19*

Distortions in our religious traditions have promoted the mistaken idea that it is somehow bad—perhaps even dangerous—to love ourselves "too much." Popular misconceptions abound about God wanting us to think little of ourselves in order to be favored and approved. Don't the scriptures tell us that "those who humble themselves will be exalted"(Luke 14:11)? The problem comes in how we understand humility. Our English word "humility" is linked to the root word "humus" meaning earth, ground. It means being planted in the Ground of our Being, knowing ourselves to be rooted in our creaturehood, needing first to receive love before we can give it. Unfortunately certain misguided religious teachings have given us a shame-based idea of humility. In the words of a song from "My Fair Lady," it's often "not the earth the meek inherit, but the dirt." Humility becomes linked with a sense of shame while a healthy love of self is confused with self-absorption and self-centeredness. Yet the opposite is the case: the more we are able to love and respect ourselves as a gift from God, the more we are able to love others. This was wonderfully demonstrated by Sarah, the three and a half year old daughter of friends, who unabashedly declared her love for herself during her bedtime prayers. As she and her mother were saying their evening prayers, she stretched out her arms as wide as she could and said, "I love Daddy *this* much!" Then, "I love Mommy *this* much! And then—"I love myself *this* much!" Her mother filled with tears to see her daughter loving herself so freely—in a way she had not been able to as a child. She saw in the fresh exuberance of her daughter the precious gift that so many of us lose so early: the passionate love of ourselves rooted in the goodness of creation.

Self-hatred is a serious and destructive spiritual malady. Because it so often masquerades as goodness—as humility, love of others, avoidance of attention, etc—it is often difficult to recognize self-hatred and its harmful effects. We tolerate its insidious presence, mistaking it as a virtue while it undermines our healthy love of self. As a psychotherapist, I frequently point out to clients the great price they pay for their self-hurting attitudes and behaviors. For example:

- A woman wins an award but immediately disparages her own accomplishments.
- A man refuses to develop his own talents, wallowing in passivity and resentment.
- A person prides herself on forgiving others, yet refuses to forgive herself for falling short of her own expectations.

We often do not recognize these actions as self-hating because they are so ingrained and unconscious. But as we become more aware of the ways in which we undermine and hurt ourselves, we can develop greater compassion toward ourselves. I sometimes point out to clients that they would be outraged if they saw someone hurting another person in the way they hurt themselves!

Ultimately, our attack upon ourselves is an attack upon God, a refusal to accept the self which God has made. There is an Hasidic saying that a host of angels goes in a vanguard before every human being crying out, "Make way! Make way for the image of God!" When we attack ourselves, we are attacking the image of God within us, an image we are called to treasure and nourish in ourselves and others.

The Scottish psychoanalyst W.R.D. Fairbairn believes that our self-hatred can also be a way of "keeping mother or father good." As children we are radically dependent on our parents and so need to see them as good and

dependable. The thought of being dependent on a parent who is unpredictable, unloving, perhaps even abusive, is so frightening that the child instead idealizes the parent—keeps mother or father "good"—while taking the parents' badness into the self where the child tries to control this badness by making it his or her own. The child's reasoning says: It is better for me to be bad than for my parents and, by extension, the whole world to be bad. As Fairbairn puts it,

> It is better to be a sinner in a world ruled by a good God, than to live in a world ruled by the Devil. A sinner in a world ruled by God may be bad; but there is always a certain sense of security to be derived from the fact that the world around is good.... In a world ruled by the Devil...[we] can have no sense of security and no hope of redemption.[17]

Self-hatred can also be fueled by an unrealistic perfectionism. A young woman described it this way: "I feel as though I'm either on a pedestal or in the pit. I believe no one will love me unless I am perfect, but when I fail, I feel utterly worthless." As she explored the hurtful consequences of these irrational extremes, she came to see that her "pedestal" and her "pit" were actually both manifestations of her underlying desire to control reality and shape it to her will. Only as she began to relinquish her idol of absolute control could she begin to accept herself and others as a mixture of weakness and strength. Only by abandoning both her pedestal and her pit could she simply "join the human race," knowing that she had infinite worth simply because she existed, not because of her own impossible standards.

Our self-hatred is a refusal to accept our preciousness in God's sight, substituting our own self-absorbed judgment for God's mercy. We turn a withering judgment upon ourselves, refusing to have what Francis de Sales calls "meekness toward ourselves":

> Many people...when overcome by anger...become angry at being angry, disturbed at being disturbed, and vexed at being vexed. By such means they keep their hearts drenched and steeped in passion. It may seem that the second fit of anger does away with the first, but actually it serves to open the way for fresh anger on the first occasion that arises.... We must be sorry for our faults in a calm, settled, firm way.[18]

Repenting of our self-hatred involves dethroning ourselves from the ultimate judgment seat, extending to ourselves the same mercy we would extend to others. In one of his poems, Gerard Manley Hopkins ponders his own lack of mercy on himself:

> My own heart let me more have pity on; let
> Me live to my sad self hereafter kind,
> Charitable; not live this tormented mind
> With this tormented mind tormenting yet.[19]

Feelings of self-hatred may masquerade as false humility. We can project our self-thwarting attitudes onto God, thinking God expects us to put ourselves down. Any stirrings of self-love are squashed because we think they take us away from God's will. God then becomes an ogre who delights in thwarting our natural desires and we become self-loathing doormats. But when we let ourselves be loved, we discover that we are accepted as we are. Paul Tillich speaks of how we often become aware of God's liberating acceptance when we are feeling most trapped in our self-hatred and self-frustration:

> Sometimes at that moment a wave of light breaks into our darkness, and it is as though a voice were saying, "You are accepted. You are accepted by that which is greater than you, and the name of which you do not know. Do not ask for the name now; perhaps you will find it later. Do not try to do anything now; perhaps later you will do much. Do not seek for anything; do not perform anything; do not intend anything. Simply accept the fact that you are accepted. If that happens to us, we experience grace.[20]

Grace breaks in when we least anticipate it. God's love is stunning, disorienting as it streams into our darkness, accepting us as we are. As we open to love, we find something surprising: instead of ironing out the wrinkles of our character—our neurotic wounds, our anxieties, our peculiar psychic dead-ends—love comes to enliven us *as we are.* We are breathed into by the Spirit of Life, set upon our feet to stand before God and the world in all the glory and vulnerability of our true selves. We had imagined we would become some other sort of person—that we could escape the bedeviling flaws of our character. Instead, we discover that those "flaws" are the very openings through which love can touch us to the core of our being.

Prayer

Forgive me, my God,
for not loving myself
as I ought.
I have failed to treasure myself,
to have compassion on myself.
I have failed to recognize
my acts of self-hatred,
rationalizing them as necessary,
even good and holy.
Teach me to love myself,
to respect my infinite
preciousness,
for in loving myself
I honor you.
In venerating your sacred presence
within me,
I venerate your presence
in all things.

−Phillip Bennett

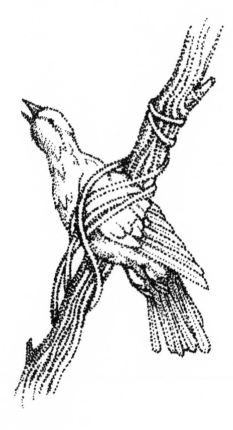

Chapter Seven
The Fear of Joy

"What does it matter whether a bird be tied to a stake by a rope or by a slender thread, so long as it is tied and cannot fly?"

—John of the Cross

Why would anyone fear joy? It seems absurd. Don't we all desire joy? As strange as it seems, I have found in myself and others both a desire and a fear of joy. This fear of joy can be another obstacle to letting ourselves be loved. We frequently express our fear of joy in phrases like, "Things are going too well; I'm waiting for the other shoe to drop; If I'm too happy I'll tempt the Fates; If I'm too successful I'm afraid I will have to pay for it; I feel guilty for enjoying my life when others are suffering so much." These phrases express a fear that joy is risky because it may be cut off at any time. Better to live with the volume turned down and one's expectations lowered than to experience joy to the full, only to have it snatched away.

Fear of joy sometimes signals the presence of what family therapist Ivan Boszormenyi-Nagy calls "invisible loyalties."[21] Our loyalty to family members—especially those who are unhappy and wounded—makes us feel as though we are abandoning them in their misery if we move on and have a full and joyful life.

I once heard a rabbi tell of a man in his congregation who came to unburden himself of the guilt he felt over surviving his brother. As young men he and his older brother had been interred together in a Nazi concentration camp. His brother had devised a plan of escape in which they would scale the large wall surrounding the prison. On the day of their planned escape, the younger brother watched in horror as his brother went ahead of him and climbed onto the wall only to be instantly electrocuted. Years after the younger brother had been freed by the Allied forces and had moved to America, he still felt as though he had no right to live his life since his brother's life had been cut short so tragically. The rabbi assured him that he was in no way guilty of his brother's death and that his brother would not begrudge him his happiness. But the man's guilt persisted. Several months after visting the rabbi he had a heart attack and required heart surgery. His doctors gave him a hopeful prognosis but were puzzled when he seemed to be slipping into a post-operative coma. By all medical reasoning, he should be recovering, yet each day he seemed to be moving closer and closer to death. During one of his hospital visits, the rabbi asked to spend some time alone with the man. He held his hand and told him that it was time to let go of his brother, that his brother did not begrudge him his life, that it was time to stop carrying his dead brother on his back. He told the man that his family needed him; it was time to let the dead go and return to the land of the living. The next day the man rallied and soon returned to a fully active life.

Our invisible loyalties bind us not only to the dead but also to the living. If my parents are unhappy or self-thwarting, who am I to leave them behind after all they have done for me? How can I abandon them to their suffering and move on with my own life? It is a painful thing to surrender our loved ones to God's care, knowing that we are not called to sacrifice our own growth in order to make them whole. If we make such a misguided self-sacrifice we unconsciously perpetuate our family legacy of self-enfeeblement and unlived life. Sometimes parents themselves send out guilty mixed messages that say "I am so proud of you, but here I am left behind while you do what I never could." Unconscious or "invisible" loyalties make us keep our foot on the brake, afraid to surpass our wounded parents. To the degree that we transfer our experience with our parents onto God, we fear that God will also begrudge us our joy and will drop the "next shoe" on us just when we are feeling most joyful and alive.

When my friend Benedict suggested that I replace my tape recorder image of God with an image of God delighting to be with me, something in me recoiled, thinking this was "too good to be true." As I sat in the stillness, I kept expecting the "other shoe to drop." Something bad was bound to happen if I sat alone with God. If I felt too good, God would begrudge me my joy. Such a view of God has more in common with the Greek gods who felt threatened by mortals' successes than the God proclaimed in the words of the early Christian theologian Irenaeus: "The glory of God is the human person fully alive."[22]

Besides our fear of surpassing those we love, we may fear joy simply because it is new, spacious and unfamiliar. Like a caged animal that has grown used to its confined world and does not venture far once set free, we become accustomed to living small, predictable lives without zest and delight. But this is not the vision of life held out in John's Gospel where Jesus prays that we "may have life and have it to the full" (John 10:10) and that his joy may be made complete in us (John 17:13). Letting ourselves be loved means opening ourselves to the fullness of life with all its joys and sorrows, beauty, hilarity, tenderness, heights and depths.

The fear of joy is—like most of our fears— stubborn and irrational. We cannot get rid of it simply by telling ourselves it makes no sense. The old inner voices of fear and hidden loyalty continue to echo within us. When beset by these joy-denying voices within us, we need to listen to the voice of Love that is stronger than our shame and fear, reminding us that no matter what next "shoe" of circumstance may drop, God never begrudges us our joy.

Prayer

My God,
I have feared joy.
I have held back from
the fullness of life,
bound by invisible threads
of old loyalties.
I have imagined that you
begrudge me my joy and fulfillment,
that you would intentionally
disrupt my happiness,
stifle my freedom,
rein in my delight.
Now I see that you
have always been calling me forth
like Lazarus from the tomb:
"Untie him and let him go!"
You desire the fullness of
life for me,
abundant, overflowing.
Unbind me, free me for joy,
that I may be fully alive.
You have held nothing back from me.
Help me to hold nothing
back in this life,
to live it to the fullest,
to drink deeply of joy—
your joy which you desire
to share with me forever.

—Phillip Bennett

Conclusion
Fears—Lifetime Companions

All these fears—of old wounds, judgment, loss, merger, self-enlargement, loving ourselves, joy—will be lifetime companions in one way or another. We will never outgrow our fears completely; they will return again and again. Our fears are a given, a part of our humanity. Instead of trying to control our fears, we need to pray out of the depths of them, to embrace our poverty of spirit, our continual need for strength and reassurance. When we try to quell our fears through our own defensive maneuvers—through denial, worrying, overcompensating, distraction, trying to earn approval—we only give our fears more power. But when we realize that our need for love is at the root of all fears, we can open ourselves to the inflowing of love, letting ourselves be loved as we are, not as we would wish to be. We can return to the amazing truth that God longs to give us "infinitely more than we can ask or imagine" (Ephesians 3:20).

Epilogue
The Great Round Dance of Love

"Love is a conversion to humanity...the choice to experience life as a member of the human family, a partner in the dance of life."
—*Carter Heyward*

In the non-canonical scripture, "The Acts of John," [23] Jesus dances with his disciples the night before his arrest. He stands in the middle while they join hands and circle round him. He tells them, "Whoever does not dance does not know what is coming to pass." Like a wheel spinning around its hub, they dance round and round while he sings to them of his coming death and resurrection. They form a living mandala: hand in hand, in the great Round

Dance of Love, with the dying and rising Christ at the center, singing to them of inevitable loss and gain.

Dance is a wonderful symbol for connection and separateness. When we dance we touch, we synchronize movements, yet we also allow space for each other. Too much space between us and our dance becomes isolated solos; too little space between us and we step on each other's toes. Who does not remember those first dance classes when we struggled to learn how to lead *and* to follow? Dancing can be awkward; we can hurt each other, pulling and pushing. In our daily dance of intimacy with spouses, family, community, friends, we step on each other and we get stepped on. Sometimes anger and fear threaten to break our circle; we lose our balance and our loving turns from dance to battle. But there are also the graced moments when we feel ourselves moving together: the dinner where everyone is laughing, relaxed, glad to be together; the roughhousing or snuggling with lovers, children, pets; precious, unexpected moments when we feel ourselves in tune with Creation, dancing with life, neither pushing nor pulling. At these moments we embody the great Dance of Love where there is room for all. We move together, learning to synchronize our movements so that we dance with a shared grace.

When trying to describe the dynamic life of the Trinity, some early theologians employed the Greek word "perichoresis," meaning "to dance around." The Trinity is that loving energy at the heart of reality which forms an endless circle of dance, each person distinct and yet all forming a greater whole. Picture the huge, exuberant

Matisse cut-outs of dancers whirling hand in hand, and you have an image of the Trinity!

The image of dancing in a circle expresses a mysterious truth about love: the more we give love the more we receive it, and the more we receive love the more we give it. At times we have to rouse ourselves to love others, moving beyond our own negativity and self-preoccupation. We must push ourselves "beyond ourselves" in order to love. At other times we are not able to "get beyond ourselves"; we are overwhelmed by crisis, illness, stress, grief. At these times, we need someone to reach out to us, to do for us what we cannot do for ourselves. Throughout our lives we never stop needing both to receive and to give love. If we imagine that we are more in need of either giving or receiving love, we still have not understood the divine economy of love. Both the giving and the receiving are really part of a seamless circle of love in which all givers are receivers and all receivers are givers. This is what the symbol of the Trinity expresses: God is an unending circuit of giving and receiving in which all are in need and all respond to need. But we often prefer to be givers of love instead of receivers, for in that way we try to remain in control and avoid our vulnerability. Always being the giver means we must refuse others' gifts, and this, says professor of church history Roberta Bondi, deprives others of the joy and satisfaction of knowing that their love can touch us:

> It is hard to explain to a loving person who can
> only give, what [the] refusal to receive does to the

would-be givers.... The turning away of a gift destroys the reciprocity of love. In place of mutuality, it sets up a hierarchy of love that makes the one who always receives and whose gifts are refused feel empty, powerless, and incompetent to love well, and so unable to receive from the beloved with a grateful heart.... This is not, however, the baby Jesus, who receives gifts of gold, frankincense and myrrh, or the adult Jesus, either, who receives the gift of perfume from the woman who pours it over his feet....[24]

In the dance of love there is radical equality: all are both active and receptive, both subject and object, both lover and beloved.

Each day brings a new invitation to dance with Love. As we face the unknown hours that lie before us, the demons of anxiety and expectation assault us. They trouble us with projected scenarios of imagined problems: What will I do if *this* happens? How will I deal with this difficult person? There is no way to anticipate the challenges of each day. Our worst fears will rarely prove to be accurate. Our most delicious fantasies will rarely come to pass. Things may be much better and much worse than we imagine. The daily dance of love cannot be learned ahead of time; the steps must be taken one at a time. We are tempted to skip over a step to get to the part where we think we will be more secure. But the dance cannot be rushed, nor can it be slowed down. It has its own pace. As we dance we find ourselves surprised by love. An unexpected person, event, or insight transforms the whole day and we see the world with new eyes. What we feared has not come to pass, and what we thought was certain has proven transitory. But between what seems transitory or certain is the ceaseless dance which holds all life together.

In letting ourselves be loved we take the hand of every other creature and circle around the Mysterious Center. It is a great paradox of human growth that the more we discover ourselves, the more open we become to all of life. The journey "inward" leads us to that point of intersection where we realize our vital connection with all of life. We are continually being summoned to play our part, to embrace our life's work more completely and, in the process, touch others' lives more deeply. The vocation to fulfill our own potential and the call to love others is one and the same. Learning to join hands with all of creation in the Divine Dance is exactly why we are here. It is only in this Dance that we find life's deepest meaning. In the swirling choreography that links quarks to galaxies, we each have our part to play in this amazing performance.

In letting ourselves be loved, we return to our true Center, surrendering our fears again and again, discovering a new strength rising up within us even as our old false confidence falls away. At the very point of failing at our own self-invented fantasies of success, power and control, we find a small opening into the Greater Life—the narrow entrance through which we pass into the vast spaciousness of Love.

Appendix

A Meditation on Letting Yourself Be Loved [25]

*S*it quietly in a comfortable position. Let yourself relax, gently allowing yourself to enter the silence. Begin to recite the following phrases, letting their meaning sink in slowly:

> *God, I am your Beloved,*
> *made in your image.*
> *You delight in being with me*
> *as I am.*
> *Enfold me in your presence;*
> *shower me with your tenderness*
> *and unconditional love.*

Allow the truth of these words to touch you. Open your heart and let God love you. If distractions, worries or other thoughts come, simply let them be, returning your awareness to God's love for you in the moment. If you find it difficult to focus these thoughts on yourself, imagine that you are someone else looking at you. Pray these words for yourself as you would for someone else you love.

Pray this prayer regularly, letting the awareness of God's love permeate you. Do not worry about feeling or experiencing anything in particular. Whatever happens or doesn't happen is your own prayer. In time, try extending the prayer toward others, beginning with those close to you. Bring to mind someone you love and pray the prayer for him or her:

> *N. is God's Beloved,*
> *made in God's image.*
> *God delights in being with N.*
> *as she or he is.*
> *Enfold N. in your presence;*
> *shower N. with your tenderness*
> *and unconditional love.*

In time, try praying this prayer for others beyond your immediate circle, until you can extend it to people you find hard to love. Continue to pray this prayer regularly for yourself and others. You can pray it anytime, anywhere: in the car, at work, in a crowd, while looking at a stranger. As you embrace the reality of being loved unconditionally, notice how your perception of others changes. The eyes of Love which gaze at you are the same eyes with which you will gaze upon others.

Notes

1. *Four Quartets*, T.S. Eliot. New York: Harcourt, Brace & World, 1943, p. 57.

2. "Adolescence and the Stewardship of Pain" in *The Clown in the Belfry*, Frederick Buechner. San Francisco: Harper Collins, 1992, pp. 83-104.

3. *The Wounded Healer*, Henri Nouwen. Garden City, NY: Image Books, 1979.

4. See, for example, *The Interior Castle*, Teresa of Avila. New York, NY: Paulist Press, 1979, pp. 172ff., where Teresa describes God residing in the seventh, innermost "dwelling place" of the soul. Also *Showings*, Julian of Norwich. New York, NY: Paulist Press, 1978, pp. 286ff. Julian affirms that "the place Jesus takes in our soul he will never depart from."

5. *The Restoration of the Self*, Heinz Kohut. New

York: International Universities Press, 1977. For an accessible introduction to Kohut's thought, also see "Heinz Kohut's Self Psychology" by Howard S. Baker and Margaret N. Baker, in *The American Journal of Psychiatry*, 144:1, January 1987, pp. 1-9.

6. *Addiction and Grace*, Gerald May. San Francisco: Harper and Row, 1988, pp. 3ff. May provides an excellent discussion of attachment and self-image.

7. *The Voyage of the Dawn Treader*, C.S. Lewis. New York: Harper Trophy, 1994, pp. 82-98.

8. *A Secure Base*, John Bowlby. New York: Basic Books, 1988. See also his *Attachment and Loss* (three volumes). New York: Basic Books, 1980.

9. *The Gifts of Suffering*, Polly Young-Eisendrath. Reading, MA: Addison-Wesley, 1996, p. 43.

10. *Godric*, Frederick Buechner. HarperSanFrancisco, 1980, p. 169.

11. Ibid., p. 171.

12. "The Capacity To Be Alone" in *The Maturational Processes and the Facilitating Environment*, D.W. Winnicott. New York: International Universities Press, 1965, pp. 29-36.

13. *Family Therapy in Clinical Practice*, Murray Bowen. New York: Jason Aronson, 1978.

14. *Poverty of Spirit*, Johannes B. Metz. Mahwah, NJ: Paulist Press, 1968.

15. *Poetical Works*, John Donne. New York: Oxford University Press, 1968, p. 299.

16. *Your God Is Too Small.* J.B. Phillips. New York: Macmillan, 1964.

17. *Psychoanalytic Studies of the Personality*, W.R.D. Fairbairn. London & New York: Tavistockl/Routledge, 1952/1990, pp. 66-67.

18. *Introduction to the Devout Life*, Francis de Sales. New York: Image Books, 1989, pp. 149-150.

19. *Selected Poems of Gerard Manley Hopkins.* New York, Oxford: Oxford University Press, 1995, p. 156.

20. "You are Accepted" in *The Shaking of the Foundations*, Paul Tillich. New York: Charles Scribner's Sons, 1948, pp. 153-163.

21. *Invisible Loyalties*, Ivan Boszormenyi-Nagy and Geraldine Spark. New York: Brunner/Mazel, 1984.

22. Irenaeus of Lyons, *Adversus Haereses*, IV. 34.

23. *New Testament Apocrypha, Vol. 2*, Edgar Hennecke, ed. Philadelphia: Westminster, 1964, pp. 227-232.

24. *Memories of God: Theological Reflections on a Life*, Roberta Bondi. Nashville: Abingdon Press, p. 184.

25. For a variation of this prayer drawn from the Buddhist tradition of "meta" or "loving-kindness" meditation, see *A Path With Heart*, Jack Kornfield. New York: Bantam Books, 1993, pp. 19-21.

ILLUMINATIONBOOKS

Other Books in the Series

Little Pieces of Light...Darkness and Personal Growth
  by Joyce Rupp

Lessons from the Monastery That Touch Your Life
  by M. Basil Pennington, O.C.S.O.

As You and the Abused Person Journey Together
  by Sharon E. Cheston

Spirituality, Stress & You
  by Thomas E. Rodgerson

Joy, The Dancing Spirit of Love Surrounding You
  by Beverly Elaine Eanes

Every Decision You Make Is a Spiritual One
  by Anthony J. De Conciliis with John F. Kinsella

Celebrating the Woman You Are
  by S. Suzanne Mayer, I.H.M.

Why Are You Worrying?
  by Joseph W. Ciarrocchi

Partners in the Divine Dance of Our Three Person'd God
  by Shaun McCarty, S.T.

Love God...Clean House...Help Others
by Duane F. Reinert, O.F.M. Cap.

Along Your Desert Journey
by Robert M. Hamma

Appreciating God's Creation Through Scripture
by Alice L. Laffey